tē´chər/

res, guides,

vates; tireless

D0611060

Teacher

Teacher

Mitchell Uscher
Designed by Diane Hobbing

ARIEL BOOKS

**Andrews McMeel
Publishing**

Kansas City

ISBN: 0-7407-3369-9

Library of Congress Control Number: 2002111880

Teacher

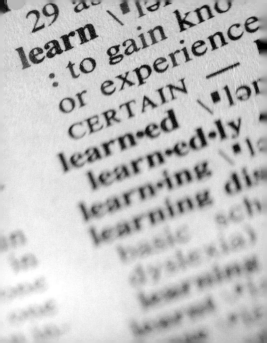

29 as

learn \ ˈlər

: to gain kno

or experience —

CERTAIN \ ˈlər

learn·ed \ ˈlər

learn·ed·ly \ ˈlə

learn·ing

learn·ing di

basic   sch

dyslexia)

learning

Introduction

There are very few people more important than our teachers. In addition to teaching reading, writing, and arithmetic, the best ones make us want to keep learning long after we have left the classroom. They help us develop patience, a sense of humor, and skills of all kinds. They teach us how to become the people we want to be—and their influence lasts throughout our lives.

There are certainly teachers we will always remember. And, in retrospect, the most important lesson we learned from them was most likely not in the textbooks. It was the example they set by being the people they were that we remember most.

The stories and quotations col-

Teacher

lected in this little book cele-brate the gifts—both small and large—we receive from teachers.

. . . you can be

cool,

Sexy,

and hip and be

educated.

–HILL HARPER

11

Beauty fades, but dumb? Dumb is forever.

—JUDGE JUDY,
QUOTING HER FATHER

Housework is a breeze. cooking is a pleasant diversion. putting up a retaining wall is a lark. but teaching is like climbing a mountain.

—Fawn M. Brodie

. . . .

Teacher

Nature gave men two ends–one to sit on, and one to think with. Ever since then man's success or failure has been dependent on the one he used most.

—ROBERT ALBERT BLOCH

No one has *ever* had these dying words:

Teacher

"I think I Learned too much."

—HOLLY STIEL

the
Lesson

My professor, paul cubeta, not only taught college courses, he taught me about myself as well.

we had a major paper to do and each of us had to meet with Dr. cubeta to discuss

our topic before we could
start writing it. I had
thought long and hard
about my theme and felt
confident as I explained
it to him.

when I was finished, Dr.
cubeta looked at me and
said, "That would make a

Teacher

very good paper–but why don't you come up with a topic that will *inspire* you to write an *outstanding* one?"

It took me forever to come up with another idea. when I finally did, Dr. Cubeta gave his approval. I never worked harder on a paper. i not only wanted to show him i could do it but i wanted to *prove* it to myself as well.

when i got my paper back, there was an *A* on top of the page—one of the very few that were given. i felt

Teacher

a sense of accomplish-
ment but, more important,
I have tried to challenge
myself ever since.

—MITCHELL USCHER

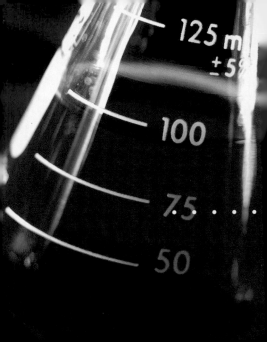

We must view young people not as empty bottles to be filled, but as candles to be lit.

—Robert H. Shaffer

Children ask better questions than do adults. "May I have a cookie?" "Why is the sky blue?" and "What does a cow say?" are far more likely to elicit a cheerful response than "Where's your manuscript?" and "Who's your lawyer?"

—Fran Lebowitz

Teacher

Teachers
reaLLy make
Lives happen
when they do
their thing.

—AL PACINO

Teacher

My hero growing up was my fifth-grade teacher. she **motivated** me to **beLieve** in myseLf, to be confident . . .

—HALLE BERRY

What you

give

of yourself is

price

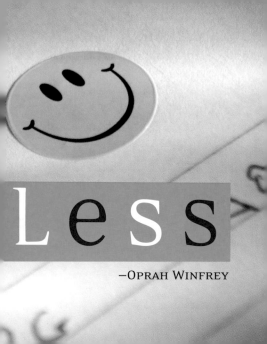

Less

—Oprah Winfrey

A well-furnished mind is a

Teacher

very
nice
pLace
to Live.

—BARBARA GRAHAM

I had a terrible
education. I attended
a school for
emotionally
disturbed teachers.

—WOODY ALLEN

◀ • • • • • • • • • •

Teacher

In a completely rational society, the best of us would be teachers and the rest of us would have to settle for something else.

—LEE IACOCCA

• • • • • • • • • • ►

A Life is not important except in the impact it has on others. . . .

—Jackie Robinson

Teacher

The best thing for being sad . . . is to Learn something.

—T. H. WHITE

Education is the most **powerful** **tool** you can have.

—GENE SIMMONS

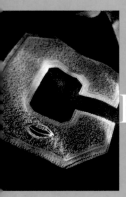

hiLdren

Teacher

must be taught how
to think, not what
to think.

—MARGARET MEAD

Any definition of a successful Life must include service to others.

—George H. W. Bush

Teacher

No matter what accomplishments you make, somebody helps you.

—ALTHEA GIBSON DARBEN

[My teacher] gave me permission to color outside the Lines at a time when the world didn't think that was a terrific Lesson for Little girls.

—Regina Barreca

much ado
about
teaching

Aaron Kramer was my high school English teacher. Mr. Kramer was a kind and gentle man, a talented poet, and a very gifted teacher who loved poetry but loved his students even more.

Mr. Kramer made shakespeare come alive, moving around the classroom and acting every part. At the end of the term, we went to see a much-heralded broadway production of *Hamlet.* As impressed as I was with the perfor-

Teacher

mance, it never quite
equaled that of Mr.
Kramer.

Mr. Kramer spent only
two years at our school,
but he had a profound
and lasting effect on all
of us. we dedicated our
yearbook to him, and many

of us kept in touch following graduation. Later, as our lives moved on, we saw him only at class reunions every ten years.

After leaving us, Mr. Kramer published numerous books of poetry and had a distinguished

Teacher

career as a college professor. But for all his success,
he maintained that the
best years of his teach-
ing career were with us at
our little high school.

Years later, Mr. Kramer
became gravely ill.
Knowing he had only a few

weeks to live, he called one of the students and told him that he would like to speak with those students who had been closest to him.

To my surprise, Mr. Kramer answered the phone when I called. I

Teacher

told him then how much I had Learned from him and how I used that knowledge every day. He told me it had been his dream to see us all one more time–and he regretted he would not be able to do so.

It was the Last time we spoke. Mr. Kramer died three weeks later.

Our fortieth high school reunion will be held this year. Although he will not be physically present, he certainly will be with us in spirit. I, for one, will be

Teacher

thanking him once again
for sharing his gifts
with me.

—PEGGY DERVITZ

I have worshiped teachers, particularly women teachers, for years—and still do. I revered my own teachers, I have two sisters-in-law who are teachers, I have

. . . .

Teacher

two daughters who adore their teachers. I have Learned LittLe in Life, but I have Learned to appreci-ate a good . . . teacher.

—DAVID SHRIBMAN

I believe that we are always attracted to what we need most, an **instinct** leading us toward the persons who are to open new vistas in our lives and fill them with new **knowledge.**

—HELENE ISWOLSKI

Teacher

we do
what we
can. the
results
are none
of our
business.

–JENNIFER STONE

Teaching is th

greatest

act o

optimism.

–Colleen Wilcox

Sex education may be a good idea in the schools but I don't believe the kids should be given homework.

—BILL COSBY

Teacher

Treat a person as he is, and he will **remain** as he is. Treat him as he could be, and he **will become** what he should be.

—JIMMY JOHNSON

· · · · · · · · · ·

ALL
growth . . .

a Leap in the dark . . .

—HENRY MILLER

I believe in the power of the individual. I believe that one determined, skilled person can do just about anything.

—JUDGE JUDY

Teacher

A test
of
wiLLs

Richard was a student in my very first fifth-grade class back in 1964. He was **charming** and **intelligent.**

I was a bit **nervous** that first day of school, but I took a deep breath and began. All went well until I started a science Lesson about the animal kingdom. suddenLy I saw a hand waving franticaLLy. Richard apparently had a very important question to ask. with an impish grin he asked, "where do babies come from?"

Teacher

I was stunned but did
attempt to answer his
question as best I could.
Nothing more was said
that day.

When I came to school the
next morning, there was a
garden bouquet of flowers
on my desk. Attached was a

note. It read: "Thanks for answering my question. you passed the test!"

P.S. Richard grew up to be a doctor.

—EVA TOBIAS

Teacher

Bloom where you are planted.

—Nancy Reader Campio

ometimes

it takes

Longer to

unLearn
than it does
to Learn.

—HARVEY PENICK

It doesn't matter who you are [or] where you came from. The ability to triumph begins with you. Always.

—OPRAH WINFREY

No bubble is
so iridescent
or floats
Longer than

that blown
by the
successful
teacher.
—SIR WILLIAM OSLER

Book design and composition by
Diane Hobbing of
Snap-Haus Graphics
in Dumont, NJ

Teacher

n. One who ins

enlightens, m

scholar